A Handbook for Building Beloved Community

"More than a valuable handbook and guide, this little volume bears witness to decades of courageous resistance and community building. Timely, inspiring, and practical, this encouraging guide will be a gift to any group trying to meet this historical moment with informed imagination and a shared understanding that everyone does better when everyone does better."

—**Marilyn McEntyre**, author of *Caring for Words in a Culture of Lies*

"Shirley Strong's *A Handbook for Building Beloved Community* is an accessible blend of history, wisdom, and decades of frontline experience. Strong connects the inner work of the heart to the structural demands of justice, creating a roadmap for anyone striving for transformation based on shared power and radical inclusion."

—**Rachel Bryant**, Vice President of Community Engagement and Belonging, California Institute of Integral Studies

"Shirley Strong challenges us to move beyond surface understanding of social justice work toward recognition of the essential transformations, personal and institutional, that lead to fundamental change. In Martin Luther King's delineation of Beloved Community, she finds the principles she has built upon in her own work and in the guidance she provides to others. The authenticity with which she shares her story supports the reader as we reflect on our own stories and consider action. Her questions guide, encourage, and challenge us to build a community that will sustain us through these fraught times."

—**Judie Wexler**, President Emerita, California Institute of Integral Studies

"This handbook is a great resource for building beloved community through turbulent times in nonviolent ways. It offers actionable guidelines in simple language with examples from the author's wisdom of experience, along with nuggets from practitioners in the movement to address racism, bigotry, and oppression. This handbook explains the imperative of creating a world that works for all through love, compassion, and courage, and shows us how to get there."

—**Sunshine Michelle Coleman**, Senior Minister, Oakland Center for Spiritual Living

A Handbook for Building Beloved Community

Lessons Learned

SHIRLEY STRONG

WIPF & STOCK • Eugene, Oregon

A HANDBOOK FOR BUILDING BELOVED COMMUNITY
Lessons Learned

Wipf & Stock
An Imprint of Wipf and Stock Publishers
199 W. 8th Ave., Suite 3
Eugene, OR 97401

www.wipfandstock.com

PAPERBACK ISBN: 979-8-3852-6862-7
HARDCOVER ISBN: 979-8-3852-6863-4
EBOOK ISBN: 979-8-3852-6864-1

VERSION NUMBER 04/01/26

In Honor of Grace Lee Boggs

I wonder how things would be different, both interracially and intraracially, if we had been able to combine Martin's Beloved Community with Malcolm's Black power.

—Grace Lee Boggs, 1915–2015

Contents

Introduction

I WAS SITTING IN my living room watching the March on Washington and wishing I could be there. I'd just graduated from high school and was about to start college. I was one of a handful of young people from my church going to college. My parents were taking great pride in preparing to send me off to obtain the college education they never received, growing up Black in the South.

Although we didn't know it, we were approaching a pivotal moment in history. I was alone when the moment arrived. I held my breath. Mahalia Jackson sang a Negro spiritual, "I Been 'Buked and I Been Scorned," and then "Move on Up A Little Higher," a fitting tribute to the moment. The first was mournful, the second uplifting. She held the audience in rapt attention. Those songs were a promise of something more. After numerous speeches over many hours, Martin Luther King Jr. finally walked to the podium to deliver his now famous "I Have a Dream" speech. Few things in my life have moved me more than that speech. I felt a combination of pride in his eloquence and oratory and inspiration in his message. I was going off to attend a predominantly White university, and I needed courage. I couldn't contain my enthusiasm. I was lifted emotionally, spiritually, and physically right out of my chair. I was moved to tears. I couldn't sit still. I started pacing. My imagination ran rampant. I wanted to tell somebody how the speech made me feel. My parents were at work. I had no one to talk to about this sacred moment in my life. I knew no one could understand what

I was feeling or what it meant to me because I didn't understand it either. The words I remember most vividly were

> So let freedom ring from the prodigious hilltops of New Hampshire.
> Let freedom ring from the mighty mountains of New York.
> Let freedom ring from the heightening Alleghenies of Pennsylvania!
> Let freedom ring from the snowcapped Rockies of Colorado!
> Let freedom ring from the curvaceous slopes of California!
> But not only that; let freedom ring from Stone Mountain of Georgia!
> Let freedom ring from Lookout Mountain of Tennessee!
> Let freedom ring from every hill and molehill of Mississippi. From every mountainside, let freedom ring.[1]

At that very moment, I decided to devote my life to social justice work. Much later, I came to understand that the purpose of that work is to build Beloved Community. Back then, I didn't know how; I didn't know what to major in, but I knew what I wanted to dedicate my life to.

The term "Beloved Community" can be traced to Josiah Royce (1855–1916), the nineteenth-century American religious philosopher. It was a part of the popular theological vocabulary of Boston University's School of Theology during the early 1950s, when Dr. Martin Luther King Jr. was a doctoral student there. Royce characterized the Beloved Community as a spiritual or divine community capable of achieving the highest good as well as the common good.

Royce stated,

> The ethical aspect of the creed of the Christian world always will include this article: "I believe in the beloved community and in the spirit which makes it beloved, and

1. King, "I Have a Dream," 3.

> in the communion of all who are, in will and in deed, its members. I see no such community as yet; but none the less my rule of life is: Act so as to hasten its coming."[2]

Royce held that each individual should strive toward this goal of Beloved Community, and the more individuals who joined the effort, the greater the possibility of achieving it. He believed this collective effort could lead in time to radical transformation of individuals. My dream is that college campuses and faith communities can serve as fertile ground for the seeds of this work, leading to the transformation we want to achieve because this is where hope abides.

King built on Royce's ideal, especially in the last three years of his life. He came to believe that in addition to radical transformation of individuals, there was a need for a deep restructuring of institutions if the Beloved Community was to be realized.

King also believed that the "oppressed" and other persons of good will have much to say about how slowly or how quickly the Beloved Community will be actualized. He understood that this ideal would require a radical transformation of values with an emphasis on love and justice. More importantly, King believed that in this country, Beloved Community would require a radically restructured society. This would mean raising fundamental questions about an economic system that places the wants of the few above the basic needs of the many. He paid with his life for having the courage to take this stand publicly. He was killed one year to the day after his Riverside Church speech on April 4, 1968.

King did not believe that the realization of the Beloved Community would one day just automatically come to pass. Rather, he saw it as an ideal that first must be envisioned, and then consciously and intentionally worked toward. It was King's hope that in every succeeding generation, visionary people would commit their lives and resources to the achievement of such a community.

The principles that form the core of Dr. King's Beloved Community ideal include

2. Royce, *Problem of Christianity*, 360.

- the interrelatedness of all things
- the solidarity of the human family
- the equal moral status of individual and community
- equality and justice for all

In *God and Human Dignity: The Personalism, Theology, and Ethics of Martin Luther King, Jr.*, Rufus Burrow writes that King believed people must strive to be in community in a particular way. In nearly every speech he gave and article he wrote, King reasserted these principles as well as emphasized the importance of respecting each other's personhood, sharing the good gifts of the world, and working toward Beloved Community.

It took thirty years for me to return to the commitment I made that August day in my living room. I eventually became the director of an anti-racism social justice initiative. Over those thirty years, I held several jobs in higher education working with students. During that time, public focus on injustice shifted back and forth from wanting to right past wrongs to feeling the pendulum had swung too far in one direction.

Barack Obama's election to the presidency in 2008, having a Black family in the White House, seemed to be the last straw for those who felt social change had gone too far or moved too quickly. For me, although I knew we were not in a post-racial America, his election felt like the mountaintop King described in his last speech before his death when he said, "I may not get there with you, but we as a people will get to the mountaintop."[3] That moment, after the 2008 presidential election was decided and Obama and thousands of people gathered in Grant Park in Chicago, wasn't as significant as the moment I heard King speak, but it felt like we had reached the mountaintop. There were still many more mountains to climb, but it was a sacred moment, one of many in my life. It felt like the Beloved Community King referred to in 1956 after the Montgomery Bus Boycott ended, when he told Black bus riders as they returned to the buses, "The aftermath of nonviolence

3. King, "I Have a Dream."

is the creation of the beloved community, while the aftermath of violence is tragic bitterness."[4] Nonviolence, he believed, and I believe, can bring about reconciliation, significant social change, and ultimately, Beloved Community.

The following chapters provide examples of what Beloved Community looks like as well as tools we can rely on during times of chaos and confusion.

4. King, "Address at the Thirty-Sixth," para. 15.

1

Legacy

The longer I live, the more deeply I learn that love, whether we call it friendship or family or romance, is the work of mirroring and magnifying each other's light. Gentle work. Steadfast work. Lifesaving work in these moments when shame and sorrow occlude our own light from our view, but there is still a clear-eyed, loving person to beam it back. In our best moments, we are that person for another.

—James Baldwin, *Nothing Personal*

This is what Beloved Community feels like.

I created my own definition of Beloved Community almost twenty years ago, when I returned to working in higher education after twelve years as director of an anti-racism initiative, and I have been working with it ever since. As we were finalizing a report for our major funder, it dawned on us that, in spite of having financial support, community leadership, and expert training, we were able to achieve only moderate success in the communities we were working in. This led me to realize there was something missing that we hadn't satisfactorily identified and addressed. For me, that something is a larger vision of the world we want to create, an understanding of the underlying structural conditions that perpetuate injustice, as well as a clear process and tools that support our work.

For example, in almost all the communities we were working in, stories of violence and injustice and sometimes precarious survival were buried deep in the community's collective unconscious, largely unacknowledged, passed down quietly from generation to generation. The 1921 Tulsa race massacre, for example, didn't come to national public awareness until a commission on the race riot was formed eighty years later in Tulsa in 2001, and one of the few living witnesses who had lived through the massacre testified.[1] There were always people who knew the story and shared it with family members, neighbors, a barber, a minister, who made sure it wasn't lost, but it was never publicly acknowledged and shared, so it never became an official part of the story of Tulsa. The suppression of these stories has impeded the healing and reconciliation that need to take place in communities, large and small, all over the country.

In one of the communities I worked with in the 1990s, a particularly horrifying lynching had taken place seventy years earlier that remained largely hidden from public awareness—a fairly common response to trauma. It was not talked about or shared, even as part of the history of race relations within the community. Although it wasn't talked about, it was still present in the collective unconscious of the community, much like in a family where an unspeakable event stays buried but doesn't go away. It continues to have an effect on the family dynamics. Nearly twenty years later, a group of community activists uncovered this information and made a documentary film about it. In order for healing to take place in communities, as in families, we have to move beyond shame, accept the truth of what happened, and apologize, though we may not be personally responsible.

Tulsa, Oklahoma, offers another example. The community there was able finally to begin to move beyond this horrific massacre by telling the story, honoring the survivors, and memorializing

1. Summers, "Survivors of 1921."

the event in a monument erected in the Greenwood community where it had happened. I had encountered a member of that community. My first question to her, a White woman, was, "Do you know what happened in your town?" She responded, "I think you're referring to the Tulsa massacre." Her awareness made me feel she wasn't oblivious to the conditions and suffering that existed in her community, and it provided me with emotional safety for interacting. This awareness isn't to be taken for granted among people who grow up socially insulated from the trauma of those nearby. In her account of the civil rights demonstrations in Birmingham, including the church bombing in 1963, Diane McWhorter, a journalist from a prominent family, writes, "I was a citizen of Birmingham in 1963, close to the age of the girls who died in the bombing, but I was growing up on the wrong side of the revolution. I knew nothing of what was happening downtown."[2]

The work of excavating and recovering from collective trauma, coupled with nonviolent resistance of the kind that characterized the civil rights movement, lays a foundation for building a Beloved Community. For example, Martin Luther King, Jr., president of the Southern Christian Leadership Conference (SCLC), spoke of their work not just as obtaining voting rights, or other historically denied rights, but to "save the soul of America," a phrase that became a watchword for Martin Luther King Jr.[3] SCLC was an inclusive movement that welcomed everyone who agreed to the principles and practices of nonviolence. Sixty years later, that movement is still seen as having changed America and become a catalyst for the anti-war movement, the women's rights movement, the gay rights movement, the farm workers' movement, Tiananmen Square in Beijing, the Berlin Wall coming down, and other movements around the world. What was it about this movement that was so dynamic and meaningful that so many took inspiration from it? Was it the leadership of people like Martin Luther King Jr.? Was it the everyday people in the street who were making great sacrifices? Was it the violence perpetrated against the movement by those

2. McWhorter, *Carry Me Home*, xv.

3. Lee, "To Save the Soul," para. 1.

in power? Was it the media coverage of sensational events on the evening news at dinnertime? Or was it the embarrassment to the US government? What was it? All of the above. But the underlying force was a shared commitment to nonviolent social change.

Nonviolent passive resistance was a spiritual practice taught and applied by Mahatma Gandhi in Indian resistance to British colonial rule. It was sometimes referred to as soul force. Gandhi brought about a way to struggle with the British that was based on the spiritual power of truth and love called Satyagraha,[4] rather than relying on physical power that would have given the British the upper hand. The British created a salt tax, and the Indians decided to walk to the sea to collect salt so they wouldn't have to pay the tax. All over the country, people were walking to the sea. It was so powerful. It broke the back of British rule: India won its independence in 1947. Years later in the US, the New Poor People's Campaign, a continuation of the original Poor People's Campaign, uses similar principles and practices for their marches and demonstrations, which are to maintain civility, self-discipline, and respect for those who oppose them.

The work looked different in the nineties, thirty years after the civil rights movement of the fifties and sixties, as we began our antiracism initiative. But the soul force that informed the earlier movement was a necessary ingredient we were not able to fully recapture, in part because we didn't fully appreciate its significance; part of what gave that movement its power was that people were putting their lives on the line. Driving down those highways at night, those involved were never sure they would arrive at their destination.

Around that time, I read a quote from Grace Lee Boggs, who mused, "I wonder how things would be different, both interracially and intraracially, if we had been able to combine Martin's Beloved Community with Malcolm's Black power." Boggs goes on to say, "It has become increasingly clear that King's prophetic vision is now the indispensable starting point for twenty-first-century revolutionaries." She also noted, "King's unique contribution . . . enabled him to tie nonviolent direct action . . . to the vision of Beloved

4. Gandhi, *Non-Violent Resistance*, 1.

Community and thereby give the struggle in Montgomery the . . . universality that is necessary to launch a movement."[5] Boggs spoke to both my head and my heart in a way that started me on a search to find an answer to the question she raised—how would things be different?

Reflecting on Boggs's question led me to my own definition of Beloved Community, which has two components—individual transformation and institutional restructuring. Often, when we speak about Beloved Community, we focus on individual transformation and minimize the part about structural change and justice. One of the best examples of King's widening focus on human rights and on the larger structural issues can be found in his April 4, 1967 Riverside Church speech, "Beyond Vietnam: Breaking the Silence,"[6] where he explained why he opposed the war in Vietnam. King described the interconnectedness between the Vietnam War and anti-poverty programs because the war siphoned off money to fund the military that could have been used for those programs. He also focused on the disproportionate effect of the war on Black men, who lost their lives in higher proportion. Most importantly, King indicted the United States as the greatest purveyor of violence in the world. He went even further to point out that this country was aligned with dictators and the wealthy rather than with liberation movements in Central America and elsewhere in the world. He advised young men facing the draft to seek conscientious objector status and ministers to give up their automatic exemptions and become conscientious objectors as well. King said,

> I am convinced that if we are to get on the right side of the world revolution, we as a nation must undergo a radical revolution of values. . . . A nation that continues year after year to spend money on military defense rather than on programs of social uplift is approaching spiritual death. When machines and computers, profit motives and property rights are considered more important than

5. Zimmerman, *Ten Thousand Beloved Communities*, 33.

6. Available online and through the Martin Luther King Jr. Research and Education Institute.

> people, the giant triplets of racism, militarism and economic exploitation are incapable of being conquered.[7]

If we're going to get closer to achieving Beloved Community in our lifetime, we cannot ignore the larger institutional and structural changes that need to occur. But we can't bring about those changes as individuals or in small groups. We have to do it as part of a larger movement. In a culture that focuses so heavily on the individual or the nuclear family, this is very challenging. King said, "We are caught in an inescapable network of mutuality, tied in a single garment of destiny," which means whatever affects one affects all indirectly.[8] This was the mantra of the civil rights movement and a core tenet of Beloved Community.

What legacy do we intend to leave in whatever space we're in? Will we be regarded as allies? I recently heard a great definition of *legacy* that spoke to me. Dr. Frank Thomas defined legacy as the fingerprints we put on the future without concern for personal recognition.[9]

My hope is that we begin to understand Beloved Community in a very pragmatic way, not just as an ideal but as an operating system for our lives and work. Since I've spent so much time working in college and university settings, I believe those are particularly important places where Beloved Community can flourish and come closer to its realization. Campuses are places where people can explore new ideas and new ways of seeing the world. When students come there, they leave familiar home environments and are opened up to new possibilities and to ideas they never even dreamed of. When I went to college at seventeen, it changed my life forever. It opened me up to a whole new way of seeing the world. I found myself in huge lecture halls listening to speakers I'd only heard of on the news. One of those speakers was Dick Gregory, who was very well known at the time as a political satirist and

7. King, "Beyond Vietnam," 7.

8. King, "Letter from Birmingham Jail," para. 4.

9. Thomas said this in his fundraising appeal for his program on African American preaching and sacred rhetoric on Nov. 12, 2025, at Christian Theological Seminary in Indianapolis, IN.

comedian. It was a privilege to get that kind of in-person exposure as a young African American woman—so many of my generation did not have an opportunity to receive it. Although these days, they are more contested spaces, colleges and universities are important places of learning and growth for people of all ages.

A framework for the practical realization of Beloved Community should be designed to respond to new issues we are facing, new tensions, and new voices in public discourse. The question that remains is, "What vision will we help to make a reality by 'acting so as to hasten its coming'?"

SUGGESTIONS

1. Be honest about the institution's history and culture. (Brown University, for example, has done a deep dive into its historical connections to the slave trade and responded with a number of initiatives to make reparation.)
2. Don't pretend to be something you're not. Be honest about demographics, history, and challenges.

2

Put Another Leaf in the Table

I have concluded that community is the place where the person you least want to live with always lives. . . . When that person moves away, someone else arises immediately to take their place! So, I think part of being in community is always having to face ourselves in the mirror of another, frequently our nemesis.

—Parker Palmer, *The Courage to Teach*

I come from a small family. We fit easily around a breakfast table or small dining room table. But every now and then, extended family would join us. As a part of getting ready, my mother would always say, "Let's put another leaf in the table." Then she would say, "Let's get out the good tablecloth." We only used it for company. Then we would get the good china out of the china cabinet and the good silverware out of the box where she kept it. Notice the pattern: we would save our best things for company. We would never use it for ourselves. That was a basic rule of hospitality.

Laying the table was just to get ready. The most important part of the day was the food. She would prepare the most wonderful food: turkey with dressing, ham, mashed potatoes and gravy, homemade peach cobbler and rolls that sat on top of the refrigerator to rise, waiting for the last minute to bake them and serve them hot.

People would sit around the table with so much joy, laughter, camaraderie, compliments to the chef—my mother. My father and I would do the dishes. In the midst of all that, my mother would often say, “Let’s take a plate to Joe.” He was a blind man and didn’t have anywhere to go for the holidays. She would heap a big plate of food and my father would deliver it to him so he could have a good meal as well. I’ve learned that there’s always room for one more. There’s always enough food to go around, even when I’m worried there won’t be. Everyone gets fed.

College campuses, churches, and local communities are a little like that family dinner table. New people arrive in response to efforts to increase diversity by inviting in those who have historically been excluded or made to feel unwelcome. Immigrants and refugees are an obvious example. We invite them to join us in civic and cultural practices and customs that are already in place. Soon, however, we find that these new individuals may have different needs and desires that require additions to curriculum, services like interpreters and translations for second-language speakers, mentoring, staffing, trauma-informed care, and more financial support. Inclusion requires a different way of showing up.

An early personal experience that led me to reflect on inclusion and belonging occurred when I was a senior at the University of Nebraska in Lincoln. I was one of only a handful of Black students who weren’t male athletes. It was a very lonely time. The only people who really saw us were the cooks and the maids. They would smile and offer encouraging words as we went through the cafeteria lines and on the floors when they came in to clean. They were the people who looked like us and reminded us of the people back home—our mothers, fathers, relatives, neighbors, community members. Even though they did their best to make us feel seen and cared about, they didn’t have any power. They couldn’t increase our financial aid or help us deal with a difficult roommate or a faculty member who didn’t think we belonged in the classroom.

Things have improved tremendously since then. There are people who look like me and my classmates at all levels of universities from presidents and administrators to faculty to residence life staff to financial aid offices. So, the landscape has changed, but many things have remained the same. Institutions are still underprepared to welcome different learning styles, different economic and cultural backgrounds, or different levels of preparation in ways that create successful, nurturing experiences.

One of the things we've learned is that when you make room at the table for the least of these, the left out, and left behind, the people who have the greatest needs, the changes end up serving everyone. One example of that is the concept of universal design—creating, from the start, architectural features everyone can utilize easily—the person in the wheelchair, the person temporarily on crutches, and the older or visually impaired person who needs assistance are all well served by universal design. Haben Girma, a Black woman, both deaf and blind, who graduated from Harvard Law School, sees disability as an opportunity for innovation.[1] There are opportunities for growth and adaptation in all institutional settings. I was a part of helping to create gender-neutral bathrooms at the institution where I worked. In the past, bathrooms were racially segregated, now the challenge is about gender. I continued to remind people of Beloved Community as we worked to create bathrooms that met the needs of everyone. The goal was to create options that enabled everyone to feel safe and respected.

A willingness to not just invite diversity into the room but to prepare to welcome it is essential for communities' survival, continued growth, and efficacy. It remains to be seen whether institutions can adapt to demographic changes and remain viable. Can people who occupy positions of authority be more imaginative about the needs of the people they serve? Can they be flexible enough to say, and mean, "If you come, we'll make a place for you at the table"? The questions apply to every environment in which outsiders need to be welcomed inside.

1. Lee, "Haben Girma."

In her own reflections on diversity and inclusion, Verna Myers, a DEI pioneer, puts it like this: "Diversity is being invited to the party; inclusion is being asked to dance."[2] Or, as I imagine it, diversity is being asked to dinner, and inclusion is being given the good china and silverware once you get there, rather than a paper plate and plastic tableware. Of course, to pursue Myers's metaphor is to recognize that new people have some responsibility and some work to do as well. Learning the dance steps, or dinner table etiquette, is one way to move from inclusion to belonging. However, institutions, not individuals, bear the primary responsibility for increasing belonging because they have the power to change policies and practices. The starting point is always the values or ethical principles that the institution articulates in vision and mission statements, public relations materials, and websites. Those guiding principles are the first place outsiders look to determine whether or not they will be welcomed. Sometimes, once they get in, they feel they have been misled; institutions frequently fail to live up to their somewhat idealized self-descriptions. People coming in with expectations shaped by those PR materials may end up feeling they have been victims of a "bait and switch." Over time, policies and practices become entrenched and normalized so thoroughly, they escape notice. At that point, they are difficult to change or even to reassess in new terms.

College and university communities were never intended to serve everyone. For much of their history, they have explicitly excluded Black people, poor people, women, and often Jews. In 1962, James Meredith had to be accompanied by the National Guard to gain entry into the University of Mississippi in Oxford. Troops were bivouacked on the quad for the occasion. This was also true at the University of Alabama in 1963, where the governor, George Wallace, tried to prevent Vivian Malone and James Hood from entering, stood in the doorway, and declared, "Segregation now, segregation forever!"[3] Exclusion of women has its own long history. Julia Morgan, who contributed remarkably to northern California architecture, was only accepted to the University of California in

2. Myers, *Moving Diversity Forward*, 5.

3. Elliot, "Wallace in the Schoolhouse Door."

1890 after overcoming several obstacles the administration arbitrarily put in her path despite her exceptional qualifications.

Educational opportunity programs (EOPs) came into being because there was no other viable way to serve Black and Latino students. Creating campus communities that are truly inclusive is an ongoing project, no matter what the political climate. The final movement toward full inclusivity in any institution has to include transformative structural changes that lead, ultimately, to full inclusion, a prerequisite of Beloved Community.

A more proactive step toward building Beloved Community is to invite difference to the table and prepare for it, not just put up with it. Sometimes, if we are in an established community—a circle of friends, a working group, a college classroom, a church committee—we expect those who enter as newcomers to adapt; the responsibility is on them to fit in. But in a healthy, dynamic community, members understand that welcoming newcomers is a two-way street: we learn from each other, and this process leads to growth. It creates a stronger organization.

The "Continuum on Becoming an Anti-Racist Multicultural Institution," an instructional graphic, divides institutions into three phases of development: Moving from an environment in which racial and cultural differences are seen as defects to one in which they are tolerated, and finally to one in which these differences are seen as assets.[4]

Similarly, Lawrence Holben, in *What Christians Think About Homosexuality: Six Representative Viewpoints*, has defined six positions churches take with regard to homosexuality, ranging from rejection (homosexuality is against the law of God and anathema) to full acceptance, including ordination, and finally, to a recognition that people who are not heterosexual are necessary to the church's survival and spiritual development.[5]

I grew up in a church I have thought of as a Beloved Community—loving and nurturing and attentive to my needs—but I

4. Crossroads Antiracism Organizing and Training, "Continuum on Becoming," adapted from Bailey, "Theory and Practice."

5. Holben, *What Christians Think*.

have subsequently realized that it wasn't a Beloved Community for all children. I fit the image of the little Black girl with pigtails in her Sunday best going to Sunday school. I was encouraged and supported. When I didn't do well at my piano solo, no one judged me harshly. When I memorized my assigned Bible verse, I was praised. They gave me money and gifts when I went off to college. I was part of the family. But all this wasn't true for some of my friends who came from divorced homes or who were being raised by grandparents on the margins of the church community, who couldn't afford the right church clothes or whose hair was unkempt. The love flowed unequally toward those children. Most of them didn't stay when they were old enough to make their own choice. I didn't stay, either, once I recognized my Beloved Community was selective in their generosity and love.

Survival is a strong motivation for change. Now that churches have been dwindling in numbers, they may be more strongly motivated to change than in the past. Churches want to keep the doors open. Congregations aren't replacing themselves with younger members—a good sign that in the next twenty years, fewer and fewer churches will be around. This would be a great loss. The church is very needed as a refuge for the suffering as well as those who are flourishing. It can be a place of healing and community for both. Its survival, like that of other institutions in our communities, like schools, is essential for the common good.

* * *

SUGGESTIONS FOR WAYS TO INCREASE ENROLLMENT AND DIVERSIFY STUDENT BODIES

1. Offer more financial support for low-income students—scholarships rather than loans.
2. Provide more extensive advising and mentoring for first-generation college students, in particular.
3. Create ways for students from marginalized communities to get involved with organizations serving those communities.

3

Don't Go It Alone

If you want to go fast, go alone; if you want to go far, go together.

—AFRICAN PROVERB

I'M STRUCK BY ONE piece of advice everyone offers during challenging times of political and social transition: find a community—a group that can get through difficult times together. Whatever it is, don't try to do it by yourself. This advice isn't as easy to follow as it might seem. Being part of a community doesn't just happen automatically; we have to work at it. About 27.6 percent of Americans live alone, a higher rate of single living than in any other country.[1] Isolation can lead to poor mental and physical health. It's not accidental that we generally value individualism over communitarianism and competition over collaboration. We are socialized to operate competitively from early in our lives, for example, in sports and academics, where individual achievement is publicly rewarded even when teamwork is encouraged. We are not taught to be collaborative. So, when we reach adulthood, it's

1. Anderson et al., "Share of One-Person Households."

hard suddenly to work as members of a team. Competition makes it difficult to work for the common good.

There's power in groups. For example, twelve-step programs, weight-loss groups, fitness classes all provide circles of people who encourage and hold each other accountable. In churches, people come together for study and prayer, sometimes forming long-term relationships with prayer partners. Many of us have been conditioned to believe we can and should take care of ourselves and our families, but our sense of obligation doesn't extend beyond those in our immediate circle. Correspondingly, we hesitate to call on others for help. Social change is only possible when people band together in organized groups. Individuals often serve as catalysts, but the work always has to involve a larger group. Those we elevate as heroes are often just the most visible. Rosa Parks, for instance, honored as the mother of the civil rights movement, didn't undertake protest alone. She was a catalyst for a whole group of organizations, including the Women's Political Council, many of whom worked at Alabama State University and who sprang into action when she was arrested. They immediately organized a one-day bus boycott. By mimeographing hundreds of flyers to circulate throughout the community, especially the churches, to announce the boycott, the boycott was successful: the buses were empty. They voted to continue. Still, we generally credit Rosa Parks and lose sight of all the work behind the scenes that went into the successful outcome—the end of segregation on Montgomery city buses. This is just one example of many throughout history that happened when people come together to work for change. Mass movements, by their very nature, are made up of everyday people.

I grew up among those everyday people. My neighborhood was an African American community, euphemistically referred to as the "Near North Side." It was larger than my family, larger than my block, larger than my church or school. It encompassed nearly everyone, even people we didn't know personally, or even like. These days, that sense of mutual responsibility and support is no longer the norm, especially in urban settings, though it is still the case that when there's a tragedy—a lost child, a flood, a fire—people come out to support each other. Many of us don't even know our neighbors' names. If they were lying on the sidewalk, any of us would help them, but many needs go unmet and unacknowledged. We're conditioned to believe that privacy is more important than community, hence the saying, often borrowed from Robert Frost, "Good fences make good neighbors."[2]

Sometimes, oppressive or life-threatening circumstances drive people to rely on one another in ways that create a deep sense of mutual care. When African Americans were enslaved and ran away, many believed they had more chance of success if they went as a group. Many partnered in the effort to get to freedom. To some of us, this might seem odd—a partner might slow you down. But the notion that we can't—or shouldn't—depend on anyone but ourselves ran counter to the deeply communitarian culture that enslaved people, like indigenous people all over the world, inherited as part of their legacy from Africa. In the television adaptation of Alex Haley's *Roots*, Fiddler tells Kunta Kinte that the one thing slave masters want is for a slave to stay by himself alone.[3] The enslavers wanted people to reproduce but didn't encourage strong family ties. Isolating enslaved people made them weaker. Therefore, enslavers purposely created divisions among enslaved people and often forbade the practice of African rituals, traditions, language, or even music, particularly drums.

Immigrant communities often support community members' financial endeavors by means of a group-based rotating savings and credit plan. Close friends and family contribute to a money pool from which one or another may draw for starting a business or buying a home. This practice has been instrumental in bringing new businesses into under-resourced communities and has enabled not just individuals but communities to flourish, even when local banks wouldn't loan them money.

Because of community-based organizations, after the Civil War, the literacy rate among African Americans went from 5

2. Frost, "Mending Wall" in *Poetry*, 33

3. Greene and Erman, *Roots*.

percent before the war to 70 percent by 1910.[4] After the end of enslavement, colleges were created by church denominations and philanthropists to help educate and train formerly enslaved people. We still see vestiges of these practices in churches that maintain funds for helping people in need or for helping young people go to college, but much more is needed.

Black churches were gathering places for movement activities because they were one of few or the only independent institutions in the Black community. They were the bedrock of the civil rights movement in every community across the South. In Selma, Brown Chapel was the church that marchers retreated to after being turned back at the Edmund Pettus Bridge. It was where they bivouacked—their starting and ending point. They often returned bloodied and battered to receive first aid and care. In Memphis, Clayborn Temple became headquarters for the 1968 sanitation workers' strike, the event that brought Martin Luther King to Memphis, where he was assassinated. In Birmingham, the Sixteenth Street Baptist Church was a rallying point for civil rights activities. In 1963, it was bombed a few weeks after the March on Washington and four little girls were killed while attending Sunday school. Churches were gathering places for these movement activities because they were the only independent institutions in Black communities.

Unfortunately, many no longer regard churches as the center of their social lives and the primary source of spiritual and social support, especially during difficult times. According to a 2024 Gallup poll, only three in ten adults in the US attend church regularly.[5] One reason some offer for staying away is that churches are no longer meeting the needs of people who might once have seen them as a refuge. Some say they do not feel welcome; churches have inadvertently become exclusionary.

There are alternatives to traditional churches—gatherings of people who come together to sing and play music in Spirit-led, nontraditional ways. Some of these are located in current or

4. Jaynes, "Literacy."

5. Jones, "Church Attendance Has Declined."

former churches. One example is Clayborn Temple in Memphis. The Temple building is being restored and repurposed, serving partly as a place of worship but also as a performance space, museum of civil rights, and political gathering place. It was bought by a local community organization.[6] In Nashville, a young man who grew up singing in church choirs and missed it got together with a group of people and created The Choir Room, which performs in a university music studio.[7] A similar group called Old Church Basement does the same thing.[8] Such groups are forming all over the country. They are made up of people from all walks of life—young, old, all races and backgrounds—and they attract impressively talented people and make beautiful music together.

So much more is needed to build community. These are just a few examples of efforts that may take many forms. We are starved for the kind of community, real or imagined, that was once so readily available. Our souls are seeking nourishment that only intentional community can provide. It's up to all of us to do our part to reimagine and recreate community for a twenty-first century world in which we are so tied to electronic devices. Creating local chapters is not a magic bullet, but it's an essential next step.

SUGGESTIONS

1. Join, join, join!
2. Create or reinvigorate local chapters of national organizations and organize student chapters.
3. Become active in local and national faith community social justice groups.
4. Run for local government offices.

6. Clayborn Historic Temple, "Our Story."
7. Choir Room, "Hi."
8. Gospel Music Association, "Old Church Basement."

4

Tell Your Story

Until the lion tells the story of the hunt, the tale will always favor the hunter.

—AFRICAN PROVERB

IN PROGRAMS I'VE WORKED with, faculty are asked to write a statement describing the forces at work in their lives that have contributed to making them who they are—a description that offers more insight than just a resumé or curriculum vita. At first, there was resistance to that request. A few even declined, but most agreed and wrote a statement. The first year, the statements were mostly general. They didn't go into much depth about the person's life and experience. But in the second year, the faculty must have decided this exercise was useful; they wrote about who they were, where they came from, what their life experiences were, who their teachers were, and what they had learned. They wrote in-depth statements that spoke to the work they were doing and why it was important to them. This exercise had a powerful effect on the teachers. It gave them credibility with their audience. It gave the students confidence that the people who were talking with them were serious about their own growth and learning—not just about their degrees and research but about the legacies they were carrying forward.

Sometimes people feel their privacy is being invaded by such a request. It's important that people feel they can tell their stories in any way that works for them. They don't have to be comprehensive or chronological. They could start with birth, or with an ancestor's arrival in this country, or with a third-grade teacher who made a difference. The storytelling is a process, not a one-size-fits-all exercise. My experience is that over time, we get better at telling our stories, and perhaps more comfortable with doing so the more we do it. The important thing is to make an effort—start somewhere and do the best we can.

Sharing one's story with others is an intimate process—a way of honoring the work we are engaged in and the people who are there to receive what we have to give. Over the years, my story has changed and evolved. I have become willing to be more vulnerable by sharing details of my life that, in the past, I was reluctant to share. For example, my age, my divorce and single-parenting, my failure to complete my doctorate in education, my struggle through bankruptcy, and my completions—a seminary degree and buying a house in my own name after age sixty. The process of becoming more open and authentic has led people to respond to me more sincerely and generously. It's also allowed me to model the way I think we need to show up for one another in settings where we're attempting to build community. I've noticed that when I start to tell my story, and not just deliver information or knowledge, people immediately sit up and take notice. They lean forward in their seats; they start to pay attention; they put their phone aside; they really tune in and listen. I think it's because we're not used to the level of candor represented in a personal story. The more we begin to tell our stories, the more we bond with each other and create the kind of community we are seeking for both personal growth and social change.

It's hard to take risks and put ourselves on the line, sometimes even with those who know us best, because we are afraid of being judged. As Martin Luther King Jr. pointed out, we want praise; we just don't want the criticism.[1] We like compliments when they're coming in our direction. We want to be seen in a certain light. How do we get to a place where we trust one another? Sharing stories is a proven way. I always feel closer to someone when I know they've been through challenges to get to where they are. One of the questions colleges are beginning to ask on applications is, "What are some things you've overcome to get here?"

I've been a part of groups whose goal is to practice being in community, but even in those groups, it can feel as though we're in our heads more than in our hearts. Every now and then, someone will say something heartfelt, and you can see or feel what a difference that makes in bringing the group closer; but this happens rarely because of our reluctance to be vulnerable and take risks. Yet, it's the very thing we need for the work we come together to do.

There's an art, though, to storytelling. We can choose what to include. We can decide how vulnerable it's appropriate to be. We can tell our stories in our terms, perhaps organizing them around an "aha" moment, when something shifted and we saw the world in a new way. What you tell depends on who you're with: it's a gift to them.

These are some of the ways I like to start my story, since I've often been in the position of sharing it with people entering college. When I was on my way to college and feeling scared, knowing my life would change forever, I started to cry. My mother saw me and said, "You don't have to go if you don't want to. We can just turn around and go home." I was in the back seat and saw my father look in the rearview mirror. Somehow, I found the courage to say, in a faint whisper, "No, I want to go." I often wonder how my life would have been different if I had chosen to go home. Not worse, perhaps, but certainly different.

In another context, I might tell about how I was in a deeply relaxed state and, for a moment, I felt as if my soul left my body and hovered above it. From that moment forward, I realized there

1. King, "Drum Major Instinct."

was more to me than my body. That awareness has supported me for the next forty years of my life.

A third story is about when, after having an experience with a close family member who suffered from chronic alcoholism, I realized that if I didn't stop drinking, that would be me in twenty years. At that moment, I said to my Higher Power, "With Your help, as soon as I finish this last bottle of wine, I will never take another drink for the rest of my life." That was forty-five years ago. I haven't had a drink since. Telling stories like these says something about who I am, where I've come from, and the choices that have shaped me.

I have not shared all these stories in a group; I've shared them with one person at a time. But real power comes from being able to share these stories in a church service or classroom or a community event. In churches in my parents' generation, people often stood up and testified—told the story of how they "made it over" or came to faith. My mother loved a hymn that began, "I love to tell the story of unseen things above."[2] Sharing our stories is a modern-day version of that life-giving practice.

In my travels around the country, I have noticed that public art in African American communities often doesn't represent the experience of those who live there. You can talk about authenticity, or you can model it.

One of my mentors used to say, "Your role as a group facilitator is to be willing to speak what's not spoken and to say what's not speech-ripe." Either a person knows what they'd like to say but is unwilling to say it for some reason or hasn't figured out how to say what they want to say and is struggling to find the words. It's a gift to bring what is coming to language for the first time into a room in a respectful, compassionate way that can support healing both for the individual and the group. I have always wanted to be able to do that comfortably in order to advance the work of building Beloved Community. When it happens, the effect is palpable. It's a rich, delicious dessert that provides both pleasure and sustenance.

2. Hankey, "I Love to Tell."

SUGGESTIONS

1. Make a list of five important parts of your story that are worth sharing—five scenes or people or moments.
2. If you belong to a group, you might suggest that one person each month or so share a story from their life.

5

Do Your Own Work

Each generation needs to do its part to build the Beloved Community.

—John Lewis, *Across That Bridge*

As we come to the table to address problems—racism, sexism, poverty, mass incarceration—it's important to remember that each of us, and each generation, has our own work to do as well. John Lewis's reflections on his own participation in costly peaceful protest look not only back, to the march on Selma, but forward to the work to be done. Each generation has its own Edmund Pettus Bridge. Since the goal is multifaceted, in addition to wanting to change entrenched patterns, we might begin by asking ourselves where our blind spots are and how we might actually be complicit. What do I need to learn about the history of oppression and colonization to understand current conditions? Are we holding grudges? Are we practicing forgiveness? Do we listen well before offering an opinion? Are we leading with love? Inner work is heart work, not just head work: we need to be willing to be vulnerable, to step outside our comfort zones, and ask questions, including of ourselves, along with proposing solutions. Are we, in turn, supporting others who are questioning or whose assumptions are different from ours?

After working in social justice circles for over forty years, the question that continues to haunt me is, do those of us engaged in addressing these problems directly, those of us who are working with vulnerable populations, realize the importance of doing our own work together in civic organizations and faith-based working groups as well as trying to address social problems? In my experience, when we come to the table to work on issues or problems together, we tend to focus on things outside ourselves, for example, police misconduct or predatory lending practices or underfunded schools. Although these outstanding issues and many others need to be addressed to successfully change institutions, we must work on ourselves at the same time. For example, how do we honor each other's political, religious, and social differences? We don't have to change each other's minds; we just have to respect each other in spite of our differences. We can be from different political parties, on opposite sides of deeply held debates over abortion or the death penalty or global conflicts. We each can hold these views and still work for social change if we can find common ground, at least with respect to a few public concerns whose gravity most people agree on—childhood poverty or hunger or health care.

After completing a long-term project with a social justice group I was part of for thirteen years, I was reminded of an old Negro spiritual: "Not my mother, not my father. . . . It's me, O Lord, standing in the need of prayer."[1] Somehow, that sentiment works better in religious settings or spiritual communities than in justice circles; not many of us see ourselves as being in need of prayer or therapy or emotional support. Outside facilitation for working groups often doesn't address underlying problems. The lyrics of the spiritual came to mind because I realized I hadn't acknowledged my own shortcomings. Doing so would have helped me do the work with more clarity and focus. I believe if I were doing the same work now, I would lead with my heart instead of my head; I would be less judgmental; I would show more compassion; I would keep

1. McCoy, *Zion Still Sings*, 149.

the vision of Beloved Community as a high-water mark. I work now with people who have become open to the vision of Beloved Community in ways that hold us together when we encounter conflict and rupture. One of the things that gets in the way of our efforts to bring about social justice is our inability to recognize that each of us brings baggage to the table and needs support in unpacking it. We may need help in identifying and claiming our calling and in staying at our growing edges. Howard Thurman, noted theologian and mystic, speaking about the growing edge, frequently used plants as metaphors.[2] Like plants, we need to keep pushing outward and upward to expand our competencies and understanding.

When I found myself ready to move on from social justice organizing and return to working in higher education, I began to reflect on my role as a project director. I wanted to understand what worked and what didn't. More importantly, I wondered how I had contributed to the successes and failures of our efforts. Examining my own mistakes and my limitations was a painful but necessary step to my learning and growth. I realized I had not trusted my intuition and followed my heart. Too often, I had not listened to my inner voice. I had not demonstrated the courage of my convictions. I wasn't even clear about my convictions. I was clear about what I thought needed radical change: injustice, racism, bigotry, hate crimes. I was unclear about what it would take to bring about the deep institutional change that would rectify these issues—what it would take to change policies that reinforce poverty, mass incarceration, predatory lending, educational disparities, and health inequities—all problems that particularly plague underserved and vulnerable communities.

A defining moment of clarity for me was Grace Lee Boggs's speech at the University of Illinois, when she asked how things would be different today if we'd been able to combine Malcolm X's Black power (liberation) with Martin Luther King Jr.'s Beloved Community, both interracially and intraracially.[3] Her speech in-

2. Thurman, *Growing Edge.*

3. Zimmerman, *Ten Thousand Beloved Communities*, 33.

spired me to examine how we might do things differently to reach sustainable economic equity and justice. Her question seemed to be a missing piece of the puzzle. For the last twenty years, I've been trying to answer that question. Dr. Vincent Harding, a noted theologian and civil rights leader, provided another piece of the puzzle. He wrote, in retrospect, from his days in the civil rights movement that the heart of the movement had become separated from the head, and that his work was to bring the two back together.[4] These two ideas—reconnecting the head and heart and integrating Malcolm's and Martin's theories of change—led me on a search to clarify how we could work more effectively and compassionately to achieve our goals. Our challenge is to stand in the fire and have the difficult conversations, agree to disagree, and not take things personally.

Many of us are not accustomed to doing our own inner work. As social justice warriors, we tend to take care of everyone else and neglect ourselves—especially women. When it comes time to take care of ourselves, we find ourselves at a loss about where to begin. Maybe we begin slowly with simple changes of habit: taking care of our bodies, tending to our financial needs. When people put their personal lives in order, they tend to show up with less baggage and can be present in a more compassionate, attentive way. If I have to go pay a bill because I'm worried about my electricity being turned off, it's hard to focus on what's happening in the room.

Paying attention to each other's needs can be seen as meddling. I once heard a speaker offer advice to younger colleagues, and I've never forgotten it. He said, "Keep up with your life"—a simple, but profound statement. When I'm working on my taxes or paying bills, I often think of those words. It's so much easier to do this work—the work of social justice—when my personal life is in order. It's not always easy to follow that advice when we are low-resourced or living at the margin, but it makes a difference in our ability to do the work. When people are being arrested at a demonstration, they tell you, "Don't get arrested if you have outstanding warrants. You won't be eligible for release." I had a

4. Harding, *Inconvenient Hero*, 112–13.

colleague who used to say, "Now you've stopped preaching and gone to meddling." We're embodied beings. We have to build up a muscle to do the soul work.

SUGGESTIONS

1. Begin with walking more, even if it's just around the parking lot at work. Invest in good walking shoes if you can.
2. Take up practices that connect you to the earth, i.e., gardening—even community gardens. Walk in nature when you can.
3. Maintain a spiritual practice, i.e., meditation, prayer, yoga, tai chi, singing, and find and stay connected to a spiritual community.
4. Maintain consistency: even a five-minute practice once a day is more important than adopting a long practice that we don't keep up.

6

Be Bold and Tell the Truth in Love

Love takes off masks that we fear we cannot live without and know we cannot live within.

—James Baldwin, *The Fire Next Time*

It takes courage to speak the unspoken and do it gently, tentatively, and with compassion. Sometimes, you have to sneak up on the truth and catch it off guard. This is even truer for groups than it is for individuals. When a group of diverse people gather from all walks of life, different backgrounds, education and income levels, racial, sexual, or gender identities, and religions, it becomes challenging to express one's truth in love. The anxieties, resentments, and fears we hold onto, including fear of giving offense, keep us from having courageous conversations with each other, even when we're working toward the same goals. We rarely have the real conversations that need to be had. But every now and then, we get lucky, and the truth spills out almost unexpectedly. We're often surprised that we all remain at the table when this happens.

In my experience doing social justice work over the years, this dilemma is what keeps us from getting to the root causes of problems. It's important to look in the mirror at our own reflection as well as out the window. Each of us is holding back things we think would be helpful to the discussion, but too often we're afraid to share because we don't want to offend members of the group; we don't want to be seen as distracting from what some would call the "real work." Their notion of real work may not include significant attention to interpersonal dynamics. This work includes addressing the question, "Who must I be?" not just "What must I do?"

So, how do we get beyond this fear? When we're working in the social justice arena, it is important to lead with the heart. As I've suggested, we need to share our stories with the people we're working with, and those we're working for, to help them understand what has made us who we are—where we're coming from. In these situations, a skilled facilitator can be helpful to keep things from going awry. However, even the best facilitators may be challenged and dismissed in groups whose collective trauma has made them unable to face the pain and injury they have endured or witnessed. What remains unresolved gets in the way.

There's no easy way to remove this roadblock. It's more a matter of being conscious of the common tendency to avoid doing inner work together, recognizing avoidance when it occurs, and staying with the process, even when it's painful and disruptive and appears to take us off course. One of the essential ingredients in this work is to establish a set of agreements or guidelines for the group to rely on, especially when conflict arises. Sometimes they're clear to everyone and sometimes they're not. They help us maintain the social contract. They're like the universal traffic signs used all over the world so we can avoid killing or hurting each other. I like to refer to them as Beloved Community Agreements. It doesn't matter what we call them. The content of the agreements is less important than the fact that we have them and all agree to use them. I've noticed that when we need them most—in challenging meetings, for instance—we tend to overlook them. We're less likely to use them. We don't hold each other accountable when we ignore them. Even with just a couple of people, when things go off track, it helps to slow down, take deep breaths, and look at our agreements again. When we're emotional, a different part of our brain is at work.

This work involves compromise. Complete consensus usually isn't possible, but the important thing is that we find some core values and strategies we agree on and focus on those while agreeing to disagree on others.

When I was working as dean of students and director of diversity almost twenty years ago, I ran across a set of agreements from one of the consultants we hired to do training. It was the first time I had seen agreements like these, and I thought they would be useful in a lot of different settings, so I borrowed them with consent. I had them designed and printed and made them available in classrooms and other settings for faculty and staff use. I wanted them hung in all classrooms, so they would be easily accessible and available when needed.

Some colleagues resisted using them at that point: it seemed unnecessary and a waste of time. A number of copies sat in my office up against the wall, but over the course of weeks, months, and years, faculty and others would come and ask me for them. They would say, "Do you have those agreements? I could use those in the classroom, since we've had a conflict or a rupture that needs to be processed." Now, many years later, we have redone those same agreements, designed and printed them, and placed them in every classroom, in every meeting room, wherever people gather. It took twenty years to get acceptance, but now more than ever, people see the importance of using these agreements as a tool. We now call them Beloved Community Agreements. What is important is that communities create and use similar agreements that pertain to their own situations. These offer a prototype. It shouldn't take too much time to adapt or detail them for new purposes.

Cornell West has often reminded us that "justice is what love looks like in public."[1] Working toward justice is love work. Sometimes we lose sight of the care, compassion, and respect that keep a community healthy when we're doing justice work. Josiah Royce, who first used the term "beloved community," said that

1. West, "Ware Lecture."

every decision we make, every action we take should be based on whether or not it advances Beloved Community.[2] At one point, I was the elder in a group of people who wanted to exclude two people who were being disruptive and not supporting the mission and goals of the group. They kept asking me to talk to them and uninvite them. I hesitated for weeks and months. I felt somehow that approach didn't reflect Beloved Community. It got to the point where the group was really suffering. They said, "If you don't act, the group will dissolve." I talked to the people involved on two or three occasions and tried to explain what our goals were and how we wanted to work—not on their particular agendas but on those the group as a whole had decided to work on. Finally, in exasperation, I said, "Take them off the list so they don't get notices of the meetings." That worked. We never had to confront them directly. I tried, but they wouldn't listen, so we simply removed them. They had been trying to use the group for their own purposes. They would drive eighty miles one way to get to the meetings, but they weren't contributing to the overall success of the group. That decision was hard but necessary.

Acting in love can sometimes involve confrontation. If we approach it in a spirit of generosity and respect, confrontation itself can be healing.

SUGGESTIONS

1. Practice having a difficult conversation—something you've wanted to talk about but have avoided—with someone close to you—a family member or friend.
2. Practice handling disruptive individuals in meetings with compassionate empathy—looking beyond their faults to see their needs.
3. Be aware of tone of voice: notice speech habits that may make it hard for people to receive the information you're sharing (i.e., an "up voice" that makes statements sound like

2. Royce, *Problem of Christianity*, 360.

questions, for instance, or a tendency to speak sharply in a way that sounds abrupt or critical.)

4. Workshops are available to train people in methods of de-escalation. Consider taking one of these if conflict is hard for you.

7

Acknowledge Wrongdoing and Work Toward Healing and Wholeness

Forgiveness: Your health depends on it.

—Johns Hopkins Medicine Home Page

In 2001, I attended the world conference against racism and xenophobia in Durban, South Africa, ironically, just days before 9/11, an event that changed the world. I had to go all the way to South Africa, the other side of the world, to learn about a lynching of a pregnant Black woman in a town in the American South who was protesting the lynching of her husband—two events that took place around eighty years ago in one of the communities where I had worked for years. This whole conference was, at its core, about truth and reconciliation. What better place to hold this conference than South Africa, which had just recently come out of apartheid—one of the few places on the globe where a revolutionary struggle ended in a peaceful transition of power.

I was on the board of an organization that produced a film about the Truth and Reconciliation Commission (TRC) called

Long Night's Journey into Day.[1] As important as the TRC was, it could go only so far in healing the wounds of a nation. What seemed to be of primary importance to most Black South Africans was to know what had happened to their loved ones. Most Afrikaner participants wanted to avoid prosecution by admitting their culpability, although most of those who participated in the TRC weren't the people at the top giving the orders; they were the ones who followed orders.

What was striking about the film was how it showed the pain and suffering of Black South African women who had lost their husbands, fathers, sons, and other family members in the struggle. They wanted to know where their loved ones' bodies were buried. Most of all, they wanted to know details of what happened to them. Were they tortured, for example? One of the most poignant moments in the film was the wailing of Black South African women. People in the room were visibly uncomfortable, including, it seemed, Desmond Tutu himself. It's important to bear witness to people's undisguised, unfiltered pain, though seeing it, even on a screen, can make us very uncomfortable. Martin Luther King Jr. used to say that "unearned suffering is redemptive."[2] In other words, it can be restorative. Redemption can be hard-won and often a long time in coming—hence King's oft-repeated words, "The arc of the moral universe is long, but it bends toward justice," even if most of us don't live to see it.[3] Nelson Mandela was a notable exception.

The South African TRC modeled for the rest of the world how to begin healing after systemic oppression and violence. Another powerful model emerged in the US under the leadership of Rev. Nelson and Joyce Johnson, when the Greensboro Truth and Reconciliation Commission was formed in 2004—a belated response to the 1979 Greensboro massacre. Forty-one years after the massacre, the commission published its report saying that the police were negligent in not protecting the demonstration.[4] The police had in-

1. Hoffman and Reid, *Long Night's Journey Into Day*.

2. King, "Suffering and Faith," para. 3.

3. King, "Where Do We Go."

4. Beloved Community Center, "Greensboro Truth and Reconciliation Commission."

formation that the Ku Klux Klan and the American Nazi party were planning to attack the rally, but they deliberately stayed away. The report was a modest vindication for the victims of the massacre and their families; Archbishop Desmond Tutu sent a letter of support to the commission at the time of the hearings that reiterated the need for truth and reconciliation after tragic violence.[5]

I was part of a group of individuals, including Grace Lee Boggs and others, visiting sites across the country that were highlighted in a 1998 publication entitled "The One America in the 21st Century Initiative on Race" that President Clinton had formed. The Beloved Community Center of Greensboro, North Carolina, was one of ten sites we visited. Our visit coincided with the release of the TRC Greensboro report. One of the things that haunted me about my visit to Greensboro was a story I heard about the day of the massacre. When the shooting started, members of the organization planning the event began searching for a safe haven for the children who were present. Of the many who might have offered, however, only one woman opened her door to get the children to safety. When I heard that, I asked myself the question, "What would I have done?" Each of us, I think, when faced with situations where others are threatened, must ask ourselves that question.

Twenty-five years later, the Greensboro TRC helped to bring about recognition and acknowledgement of what happened to the five people who were killed during that massacre and the others whose lives were deeply affected. In addition, many other communities were also victims of brutal racial violence. Just to mention a few of those better known, Wilmington, North Carolina; Tulsa, Oklahoma; and Rosewood, Florida are sites of some of the most brutal racial violence. In all these instances, an entire community was attacked by a violent white mob.

The Tulsa massacre, which took place in 1921, was very close to a small town in Oklahoma, about forty miles outside of Tulsa, where my mother was raised. She was in her teens when it occurred, and she lived well into her nineties. In all those years, she never mentioned any of those events to me. I have no doubt the

5. Mayer, "From Fear to Truth."

trauma affected her deeply, but she never talked about it. She was uncomfortable around large groups of White people she didn't know. As an adult, my mother never wanted to talk about anything related to racial violence, or to watch anything on television that was a historical portrayal of enslavement or documentation of racial violence, like *Roots* or *Rosewood*. She often said to me, when I invited her to watch documentaries about racial violence, "I don't have to talk about that. I lived it." I never understood until later what that meant. She was traumatized, and trauma runs deep. It affected her ability to engage with others in diverse groups. Whenever she did, she would develop debilitating migraine headaches. She never shared the full story when she was alive. Now it's too late. I can only imagine what she went through. She left Oklahoma when she became an adult and moved further north rather than go to Tulsa, where her sister was living.

John Hope Franklin, a noted African American historian and chair of the president's initiative on race, was also a child during the massacre. His father was an attorney. After the massacre, his father went missing for two or three days. My mother and John Hope Franklin were shaped by this event in different ways. My mother retreated into herself and didn't talk about it. Franklin told the story to millions of people. At this point, the destruction of the community of Greenwood has been memorialized, and today, only two blocks remain of a thriving business district known as Black Wall Street. Many Black residents asserted that bombs were dropped, though the official report omitted mention of them.

The work of reconciliation continues. Trauma lasts for generations, and forgiveness is ongoing. *Without Sanctuary*, James Allen's collection of photographs taken at lynchings, many of them made into souvenir postcards, offers a grim and eloquent reminder of the cruelty deep-seated racism engenders.[6] To my surprise, one of the photographs was of a lynching that occurred on the railroad tracks of my own hometown in the 1920s. Even though I grew up there, I never heard about it, which gives some measure of how buried these incidents are.

6. Allen, *Without Sanctuary*.

There are both community pain and individual pain. Though many communities weren't demolished like Greenwood, so-called urban renewal, known in many African American communities as "urban removal," has continued to destroy the heart and soul of Black communities all over the country, including my own hometown. Pain and suffering keep showing up. Forgiving is an ongoing process.

SUGGESTIONS

1. Research the racial history of the community you live in and/or the one you grew up in and share that history with groups you are a part of: church, civic groups, social clubs.
2. Invite a local historian to share the history of injustice in the community you belong to.
3. If you're a member of a book or film club or a group focused on social justice, pick a book or film on racial or gender-related violence in the US to read together.
4. Invite organizations that focus on racial reconciliation and healing to speak to your local community.

8

Don't Demonize Opponents

He that is without sin among you, let him cast the first stone.

—JOHN 8:7, KJV

WHEN WE DEMONIZE OUR opponents, we take away from them the possibility of transformation. We write them off as beyond redemption. While Nelson Mandela was in prison, in a cell so small he could reach out his arms and touch both walls, he treated his guards with respect and regard for their dignity. Over time, they returned the same courtesy to him. Eventually, he invited them to his inauguration as president of South Africa. I went to that prison on Robben Island, where he spent twenty-seven years consigned to manual labor. It was a desolate place—a cold, foggy, rocky island off the coast of Cape Town. I believe he emerged triumphant because he was able to overcome his anger and bitterness and turn the years of imprisonment into something that worked for him rather than against him. I imagine Robben Island is where he envisioned a South Africa he wanted to live in.

Although Mandela's African National Congress wasn't committed to a nonviolent struggle, the hallmark of the civil rights struggle in this country was nonviolent direct action, as modeled by Mahatma Gandhi and taught by Bayard Rustin. This is what set the civil rights movement apart from other movements. Gandhi was the inspiration and Rustin was the tactician. The practice of nonviolence allowed participants to be viewed as heroes and heroines while their opponents were viewed as bullies and oppressors. The civil rights leaders chose the high road, which allowed the American public, as well as the rest of the world, to identify with their cause. The US government capitulated in part because they were embarrassed by the exposure of their hypocrisy in promoting democracy around the world but not practicing it at home. Over the last sixty years since King's death, our commitment to nonviolence has eroded. Still, those who remain faithful to nonviolent principles find it easier to see the people they are struggling against as opponents rather than enemies; they don't have as far to go to see each other's humanity.

The struggle has taken new forms. Over the past several decades, urban "renewal," often described by those affected as "urban removal," did severe damage to African American communities. All over the country, city planners purposefully placed new freeways where they cut right through the heart of established Black communities, dividing them in half. Overpasses took drivers over Black communities into downtown commercial areas for "convenience." Hundreds of homes—thousands in some places—were destroyed in order to make way for them. For example, in West Oakland, a thriving commercial and residential district, 800 businesses and 2,500 Victorian homes were destroyed and, according to the Oakland planning department, hundreds of businesses and thousands of homes were destroyed.[1] The final blow was struck when we reacted to injustice and police brutality with self-destructive rage that destroyed property and businesses in our own communities. Very few had access to the kind of training an earlier generation had received in how to respond strategically and nonviolently to police brutality and other forms of structural racism. Rosa Parks and her whole generation were trained at

1. Romero, "West Oakland's 7th Street"; Susaneck, "Segregation by Design."

Highlander Center outside Knoxville, Tennessee, in how to engage in nonviolent direct action.[2] Leaders and participants had to receive that training before they were allowed to take an active role in demonstrations.

I visited Highlander Center years later to pay homage to the good work that was done there in preparing civil rights activists for what they knew would be life-threatening confrontations. Highlander overlooks the Great Smoky Mountains. A long porch lined with rocking chairs looks out on the majestic view and offers visitors a place to reflect on the stories that were shared there. Highlander Center's location was not made known to many people in the area because they didn't want a visit from the Klan. One time, however, the Klan found out about the location and showed up when they were having a training. They made people get on the floor and harassed and taunted them. The trainees began to sing the movement song "We Shall Overcome." They sang and sang while the Klan yelled at them to shut up. But they kept going, singing verse after verse, making up new ones as they went. They persisted so long the Klan members got frustrated and left.[3] The trainees refused to be intimidated. The music gave them courage as they sang.

In 2015, I went to Ferguson, Missouri, for the first anniversary commemoration of Michael Brown's murder at the hands of police. He was a teenager, a recent high school graduate, whose body was left in the street for hours. The killing touched a nerve in young people who saw their peer lying lifeless and ignored in the street. The callousness of the police response—shooting an unarmed teenager—set off a chain reaction. On this anniversary, there was a Moral Monday March to the courthouse in St. Louis, along with a march to the high school from which Michael Brown had graduated. I participated in both. But before we could join the

2. Center for the Preservation of Civil Rights Sites, "Highlander Research and Education Center."

3. This story is part of oral history, widely known in Black communities connected to the Highlander Institute. It was told to me by Suzanne Pharr, director of Highlander at the time, when I visited Highlander in 2008.

march, we had to go through training in nonviolent resistance. We stood in line in a big auditorium while people pretending to be police yelled and screamed at us and insulted us. We were being trained not to react, but to remain calm and not respond emotionally. The person standing next to me was a white woman who started talking back and the trainer said, "You can't do that. They might not hit you, but they'll hit the person standing next to you who may be Black and more vulnerable." I knew from my earlier training as a teenager in the Youth NAACP in my hometown that you have to not react to provocation but use the collective moral power to influence the outcome.

When I was seventeen in 1963, the Youth NAACP integrated a whites-only amusement park and swimming pool in my hometown. I wanted to get arrested in solidarity with civil rights activists all over the country, but the police saw us as a nuisance more than a threat. Still, they changed their whites-only policy to let us in. Now, more than ever, we need nonviolent, strategically organized, and targeted protests. Today's tactics are largely the same as in the past, though sometimes assisted by electronic means, like cell phones that we didn't have then. The person who documented George Floyd's murder was a teen with a cell phone who had the presence of mind to take pictures that were crucial in evoking public response.

Grace Lee Boggs noted that King's unique contribution as a philosopher, preacher, and gifted orator enabled him to tie nonviolent direct action inseparably to the vision of Beloved Community, and thereby give the struggle the prophetic dimension and universality that is necessary for a movement. In so doing, she observes, King has also given us invaluable guidelines for movement building.[4]

4. Boggs, "Conspiracy of Hope."

MOVEMENT BUILDING STRATEGIES

- Movement builders understand that suffering and oppression are not enough to create a movement. A movement begins when the oppressed begin seeing themselves not just as victims but also as pioneers in creating a new, more humane society.
- Movement builders are able to recognize the humanity in others, including their opponents, and therefore are able to see within them the possibility of change.
- Movement builders are conscious of the need to go beyond slogans and to create programs that transform and empower participants. For example, the protestors in Montgomery created an alternative transportation system during the bus boycott.
- Movement builders believe in the concept of two-sided transformation, both of institutions and themselves.
- Movement builders are intergenerational. For example, a children's campaign saved the Birmingham protests, since many adults couldn't participate without losing their jobs.
- Movement builders can accept contradictions that develop in the course of a struggle. Great movements create hopes, but they can also lead to great disappointments. For instance, the movement was opposing racism while practicing sexism, especially in the ranks of leaders.
- Movement builders can call forth a vision that is larger than the issue at hand, widening the focus from particular social reforms to social transformation. For example, the Southern Christian Leadership Conference (SCLC), although it was engaged in the civil rights struggle, believed their mission was "to save the soul of America."[5]
- Movement builders recognize the possibility for historical moments in the convergence of time and events. For example,

5. Isserman, "Saving the Soul of America," para. 3.

> King and Baynard Rustin understood that the March on Washington was likely to be a watershed event. King's "I Have a Dream" speech on that occasion was one of the greatest in American history.

Like Grace Lee Boggs, I wonder what would be different if we'd been able to fuse Malcolm's understanding of Black power and Black liberation with King's vision of nonviolence. I've often thought that Malcolm understood and identified the problem of White supremacy and Martin understood the solution, which was Beloved Community.

SUGGESTIONS

1. With a group you belong to, create and utilize agreements for having productive conversations that enable participants to manage conflict. For example, I call the ones I use Beloved Community Agreements and include them here in the final chapter.
2. Identify one of the agreements or things you do well in groups, for example, listen or use I-messages. Also, identify an agreement that you find challenging. Share that with your group and ask others to do the same thing.
3. Think about those you may tend to demonize, at least in your mind, and consider how you might empathize with them, if only as a thought experiment.

9

Open Paths for Others to Follow

"Who am I to teach the way . . . So prone myself to go astray?"

—James Pinkney, "The Teacher"

Dr. Dawn Davis, a noted Native American social justice activist and scholar, asked participants in a 2022 training I helped facilitate what legacies they intended to leave in the social justice space and whether they would be regarded as allies. This question prompted me to ask myself, what do I want my legacy to be, given the work I've been doing for the last thirty-two years in the social justice arena? How do I want to be remembered by people I've worked with, mentored, counseled and coached? What example do I want to set for my children, and grandchildren? What do I want them to say about me and my social justice efforts? If I could write my own epitaph, I would want them to say that I was a warrior for justice—that I understood the problem was structural racism and the solution was Beloved Community. I want them to say I was a "Matthew 25 Christian"—that I was concerned about the "least of these." I would want them to say Beloved Community was the touchstone for my life and work. I lived it; I used it as the road map for everything I did.

My experience growing up during the civil rights era shaped the entirety of my life. That movement has been my north star. My entire generation was shaped by the movement. We wanted collectively to contribute by paying forward what we received, especially opportunities for higher education and employment, from the sacrifices made by previous generations who fought and gave their lives for the cause. Even today, sixty-five years later, when I see documentaries of the movement, like the sit-ins or the freedom rides, I am still deeply moved and in awe of the courage demonstrators showed during that time. This causes me to recommit my life to the work, even at my age.

In my early thirties, the first real mentor I had, the most important in my life as it turned out, agreed to take me on one condition: that I commit to passing on my learning and training to others. Her work with me wasn't purely professional; her approach was holistic. She focused on all aspects of my life—my spiritual life, my financial affairs, my role as a higher education professional, my social justice worldview. All were important to me at the time, and the spiritual grounding I received in conversation with her has served me well ever since. It became the foundation for my life. Other things sprang from that: my financial security, my confidence in my professional skills, all came from grounding in spirituality. This is what I try to pass on to others. And I try, in my turn, to work with them in a holistic way rather than focusing only on their professional needs. These days, working with women in midlife and beyond is my calling. One of the most rewarding times in my life was serving as academic advisor at a state university that served a very diverse population. People from all walks of life came through the door of the college into my office—young, old, well-to-do and impoverished, Asian, Black, Latino, and White, male and female, gay and straight, from all parts of the world. I learned to work with and serve all these various populations. My goal was clear—to get them to their degree. Often, I was the first person to show an interest in their educational pursuits. It took them a while to believe in themselves—that they could actually complete their degree.

One of my favorite memories is of an African American woman in her sixties who was a teacher's aide. She had helped educate her daughter, who had just completed a master's degree, and now she wanted to complete her BA. Together, we decided that if she was able to complete her degree and get a teaching credential, she could become a teacher and not just an aide in the classroom. She had very low self-esteem; she was especially doubtful of her ability to complete the teaching credential after the degree. However, with encouragement, including assurance from her principal that she would hire her if she got her degree, she persisted in pursuing her goal. This changed both the quality of her life and her retirement. It was gratifying to be able to help make a qualitative difference to someone who had few resources to work with.

My eight years as an academic advisor laid the foundation and gave me the skills for the work I have done since then as a dean of students and chief diversity officer and even as project manager of a social justice initiative. My work in social justice allowed me to make pilgrimages to sacred sites of the civil rights movement, like Montgomery's Dexter Avenue Baptist Church, the church King pastored during the bus boycott; Birmingham's Sixteenth Street Baptist Church, where the four little girls were killed; Kelly Ingram Park, the site where attack dogs and fire hoses were used against the marchers; the Lorraine Motel in Memphis, Tennessee, where King was assassinated; the Greyhound bus station, the historic site in Jackson, Mississippi, where freedom riders disembarked; the Jackson County jail, where the freedom riders were incarcerated; the Edmund Pettus Bridge in Selma, Alabama, where the marchers were beaten by state troopers (so hot and humid that day, we didn't walk across); Greenwood in Tulsa, Oklahoma, where the massacre took place; and the civil rights museums in Memphis and Birmingham. Those pilgrimages left indelible impressions on me and shaped who I was to become.

In Jackson, Mississippi, I went to the fiftieth reunion of the freedom riders and met people in their sixties and seventies who were in their twenties when they did the freedom rides. They told stories of their experiences on those rides and how their lives were permanently changed by that experience. They said that after that, nothing was as hard. They became lawyers and social workers and professors whose lives were defined by that struggle. Those stories, along with our own, are what my generation has to offer the next, which faces its own pressures and threats and its own version of the struggle.

My biggest personal regret is that I was unable to go to the South to participate directly in that movement. My dream was to go to Mississippi and be part of Freedom Summer, 1964. I imagine my life would have taken a different turn if I had gone. But I was eighteen and just going into my sophomore year in college. I didn't know anyone who was going, wasn't connected to any organization that was going, and I knew my parents wouldn't give their permission. I wanted to meet Fanny Lou Hamer in person—just be in her presence. She was and has been one of my "sheroes" in the movement. I tell my mentees her story, some of whom aren't familiar with her. Some of them repeat my favorite of her lines: "We didn't come all this way for no two seats."[1] The Democratic Party Credentials Committee had offered the Freedom Democratic Party two seats at large, rather than seat them in place of the Mississippi delegation, because the state party election hadn't been open and fair. They refused the offer. President Lyndon Johnson held a press conference at the same time she was speaking before the credentials committee because he was afraid of her charisma and the power of her story: she had been thrown off a farm, where she and her family had sharecropped for many years, for refusing to take her name off the voter rolls. Despite lacking formal education, she became a strong, powerful leader. She was not afraid.

One of the verses to "We Shall Overcome" begins, "We are not afraid, we are not afraid, we are not afraid today."[2] Our generation has to face its own Selma, Birmingham, and

1. Hamer, "Testimony."

2. Based on a Negro spiritual, now in public domain: https://hymnary.org/text/we_shall_overcome_we_shall_overcome.

Montgomery—its own Pettus Bridge. There's always plenty to fear. However, the fear didn't prevent the civil rights generation from confronting injustice, and it will not stop future generations either.

SUGGESTIONS

1. Identify social justice warriors from your own racial and ethnic background and find out what you can about their stories. They are often hidden in plain sight. One good source would be the digital collections at Iliff Seminary in Denver, which houses video recordings of civil rights leaders.
2. Make your own pilgrimage to sites that are important in your life, particularly those related to struggles for justice, for instance, concentration camps in Europe; Japanese internment camps in the US; the "lynching museum"—the National Memorial for Peace and Justice—in Montgomery, Alabama; the Vietnam Memorial in Washington, DC; Native American sites, like the Wounded Knee Memorial site and museum; and the Greenwood Memorial in Tulsa, Oklahoma. Plan visits to national civil rights museums in Memphis, Birmingham, Cincinnati, Washington, DC, and elsewhere.
3. Seek out and share children's books, videos, and other resources that would help young people learn about this important history.

10

Stay Connected to the Spirits of Ancestors

In times of extreme difficulty, consult the ancestors.

—African proverb

When Barack Obama was elected president, I, like many of my generation, was shocked and in total disbelief. In Chicago's Grant Park, thousands of people gathered to celebrate the evening of his election when his victory was announced. As the camera panned the audience, there were many older African Americans, tears streaming down their cheeks, including Rev. Jesse Jackson. Sitting in my living room, I was one of those people. I was crying for my parents and for family members and others who didn't live to see this day. I just wished I could see my mother's and father's faces and hear their words and respond to their disbelief that a Black man could be elected president of the United States. It would have been such a joy to celebrate that event with them. Wiser people than I felt the ancestors were aware of the moment and were looking over the balconies of heaven, trying to get a better glimpse of what was going on down here on Earth. The sense of their presence is sometimes referred to as the cloud of witnesses, mentioned by the writer of Hebrews, possibly Priscilla, in the Christian scriptures.

We need our ancestors now more than ever. We need their guidance, their wisdom, their patience, their love and compassion—all the qualities most of us develop as we age. They're available to us in times of need, with intuitive wisdom we don't always access or value, though it's always there for us. They hold knowledge for the culture and pass it on. The ancestors generally come when called. Elders are often the ones who call them in. Music, dance, storytelling, and rituals help create and maintain the connection. In West Africa, those who carry that role are called *griots.* In Latin America, they are the *curanderos* or *curanderas* and *shamans.* All over the world, different cultures have different names for them. Indigenous cultures have ceremonies for bringing in the ancestors, consulting them on decisions that affect the community. As elders, we are the community's primary connection to ancestors. The dead live in our memories.

I used to bristle at being referred to as an elder. (Some cultures have other terms to honor elders—Auntie, Sis, or Miss before the first name, for instance.) I wasn't ready to embrace, or even accept, this role. But the more I'm called an elder, most often with deep respect, the more I am willing and able to see myself in that way, offering younger generations a connection to ancestors based on my living memories and knowledge of them. Elders sometimes struggle to find a role for themselves in today's world. We're not as technologically savvy as younger people; we're not consumers of social media in the same ways; we don't have the same degree of stamina, and we process information more slowly; and our memories may not be as sharp as they once were.

One of our strengths is our knowledge of history and our connection to events younger people have only read about. We've seen enough to give us perspective on some of the challenges we're facing. For us, they're not new; they just have different players. Our gift is to provide a link between the ancestors and what we know to be true (the wisdom of the ages) and what is going on in the present moment. As elders, we may remember aspects of a

Beloved Community from firsthand experience, flawed as it was. Many of us had communities in which adults watched out for kids, and members were aware of each other's needs, though that kind of attention was not always appreciated—sometimes it felt like meddling. In many families, multiple generations lived together in one home or nearby and helped raise the children and grandchildren. Often today, I hear people in my generation say that the person who influenced them most was a grandparent. Even my children still refer to their grandfather as an important influence. But connections like that are less and less frequent. We are not as tethered.

I will always remember walking down the street in my college town with my head held down and running into a Black woman who was the cook in a fraternity house on campus, a job she held for over forty years. She stopped me and asked me how I was doing. I responded, "Not so good." I told her I wasn't going to graduate on schedule. She looked me in the eye and told me everything was going to be alright. This was a person I admired and looked up to. She sang and acted in local theater, and she had beautiful hair, prematurely white, and milk chocolate skin. Although her occupation was a cook, she was so much more than that. I wanted to be just like her. So, I believed her when she said it was going to be alright. I perked up and decided I was going to do whatever I could to make it alright. There was something about her reassurance that day when I was at my lowest point that I have never forgotten, though it was decades ago. The ancestors spoke to me through her, saying, "You can't give up now. We have sacrificed too much for you to be here. Nobody said it would be easy, but you can't give up." Not only have her words stayed with me, they have inspired me to offer similar encouragement to students along the way. I tune in to them in a way that I might not if that encounter hadn't occurred. Over the years I've thought about her and wish I'd been able to stay connected, although I didn't know her well at all. She was someone I would like to have had in my life, especially when things got difficult. She was one of those wise elders whose voice I wish I'd been able to hear again and again.

I didn't always appreciate the elders in my life when I was younger or even respect them as much as I should have. Their wisdom seemed dated and old-fashioned, and they weren't coming from a place of formal education, so I didn't see the value in what they were saying then as much as I do now. So often they have been proven right. What they lacked in formal education they had in an unbroken line of connection to our collective ancestors. As I sit in that spot now, being identified as a wise elder, I'm more willing to take on the mantle that seems to want to fall on my shoulders. My challenge is to learn how to share what I have to offer without worrying about how others accept or receive it. They may not be ready for it, they may not agree with it, the words may not suit them. That's okay. They may remember it in the future at a time when they need it most.

SUGGESTIONS

1. Practice asking questions rather than giving advice.
2. Notice when you are being judgmental, even if it's just in your mind. Ask yourself why: What's behind the judgment? Do you know enough about the person or situation to judge? Are you imposing your own cultural standards? Are you practicing "respectability politics"?
3. Make time to be in intergenerational conversation with the elders/youth you know. See what you can learn from each other.

Conclusion

"The Work"

As a reminder, my definition of Beloved Community is an inclusive, interrelated consciousness based on love, justice, compassion, responsibility, shared power, and a deep respect for all people, places, and things that radically transforms individuals and restructures institutions. This definition has drawn on the work of Martin Luther King Jr., Thich Nhat Hanh, Janet Parachin, and many others. Although it was created twenty years ago, it remains relevant for today. These ideas are timeless because they appeal to our higher selves—those qualities that are enduring over generations and that we all strive to manifest in the work we do and in the lives we lead.

According to Janet W. Parachin, author of *Engaged Spirituality: Ten Lives of Contemplation and Action*, the practice of engaged spirituality, which I refer to as Beloved Community, based on my own cultural tradition, is exemplified by a person "who finds in their spiritual tradition the resources that nurture their spiritual being and enable them to engage in activities that move the world toward peace, justice, greater compassion, and wholeness."[1] I would add to these goals responsibility, respect, shared power, and love. An intentional commitment to engage all these goals challenges us to grow by expanding beyond our comfortable boundaries, questioning our unexamined assumptions, and lifting our sights beyond our own immediate concerns. The term "engaged spirituality," she

1. Parachin, *Engaged Spirituality*, 1.

says, is borrowed from Thich Nhat Hanh, who refers to his own religious commitment as engaged Buddhism, which, in addition to meditation, involves meaningful social activism.[2] The following are ten essentials for living a life of engaged spirituality. Consider how they support us in our work.

TEN ESSENTIALS FOR BUILDING BELOVED COMMUNITY IN SUCH A TIME AS THIS

1. **A compelling experience that motivates.** My motivating experience occurred in August 1963 when I watched the March on Washington on television, where Martin Luther King Jr. delivered his now famous "I Have a Dream" speech. Few things in life have moved me more than that speech. I experienced pride in his eloquence and inspiration in his message. At that very moment, I knew what I wanted to do for the rest of my life. I wanted to work for justice and social change. I didn't know how, but I knew this was my purpose. Years later, I returned to the commitment I had made that August afternoon in 1963. I became the director of an anti-racist social justice initiative. Others have followed their own motivating moments in a wide variety of ways. Freedom Riders, Peace Corps volunteers, Freedom Summer volunteers, Black Lives Matter organizers have followed their own paths.
2. **A vision that inspires.** What has stayed with me for more than six decades since watching the March on Washington is the conviction that "the arc of the moral universe is long, but it bends toward justice."[3] I want to, as President Obama said, help bend it. The compelling experience that emerges in a lasting vision connects us to our higher selves.
3. **A spiritual practice that sustains.** I was deeply moved when I was visiting my childhood home and saw my father kneeling in prayer by his bedside at age ninety, having done it for

2. Parachin, *Engaged Spirituality*, 1.
3. King, "Where Do We Go."

almost fifty years. My father's sustaining practice is mirrored by my son's different but equally sustaining practice. A devout Muslim, he prays five times a day and has for the past twenty-five years. Each of us can cultivate a mindfulness practice that raises us above the distractions of daily life, sometimes into an altered state, and is a way of ordering our lives and providing deep connection to the universal, for example, yoga, physical exercises, spending time in nature, playing a musical instrument, or participating in twelve-step programs.

4. **A spiritual community that buoys and keeps us afloat.** For me, this relationship began in the Black church I grew up in, which offered me relationships that have sustained me for a lifetime. A relationship with a community of like-minded people can provide support and comfort through the various stages and changes of life.

5. **A commitment to others that reinforces and strengthens.** For me, this commitment was modeled when, as a young professional, I asked a woman I admired, who happened to be my supervisor, if she would mentor me. She agreed on one condition—that I would, in my turn, pay it forward by mentoring young women, especially of color. I wholeheartedly agreed and have kept my promise.

6. **A theology, philosophy, belief that guides.** Early in my life, I went on a spiritual journey in search of an ideal place, and I realized there was no perfect church or spiritual community. We are all works in progress. I heard a spiritual leader say that if there was such a thing as a perfect community, once we entered it, it would no longer be perfect. This is why I embrace the ideal of Beloved Community. It provided a way of speaking about a vision of what we would like to become rather than describing what already exists.

7. **A connection to elders/ancestors that teaches.** It's important for all of us to remember that we stand on the shoulders of the many, famous and ordinary, who came before and sacrificed on our behalf. I especially admire Grace Lee Boggs,

a social activist who was still active in her late nineties. She never sugar-coated anything. I felt intrigued by her words, "I wonder how things would be different, both interracially and intraracially, if we had been able to combine Martin's Beloved Community with Malcolm's Black power."[4]

8. **An art form that nourishes.** Artistic expression enhances our creativity and renews our spirit. Quilting, for example, has helped women maintain community and provide support to one another for centuries. In my case, collage making allows me to tell my story and the collective history behind me and has supported me on my journey toward wholeness. I did a series memorializing my first trip to the slave forts in West Africa and the Doorway of No Return. I depicted myself standing in that doorway, the last place Africans stood on African soil before they were herded onto slave ships bound for the Americas. My journey allowed me to step back through the doorway as a sign to the ancestors that a daughter of Africa had returned home. I depicted that in ten collage pieces.

9. **A gratitude/thankfulness that renews.** Gratitude is restorative. I'm especially grateful for the college education my mother was determined I should get, in spite of my lack of awareness of what it would mean for the rest of my life. All her life, she gave me things she wasn't able to get for herself as a Black woman growing up in the 1920s and 1930s in the South. At the time, I didn't have as full an appreciation for those things as I do now with the benefit of hindsight. My quality of life is so much better because of the sacrifices she made. Thank you, Mom!

10. **A sustainability that replenishes.** This includes a willingness to give back where we have received spiritual encouragement. I made a practice of keeping $20 bills in my desk drawer, and when students came into my office seeking help, I would sometimes reach into my drawer and give them money for food and transportation to tide them over until they received

4. Boggs in a lecture at University of Illinois, Champaign-Urbana, 1987.

their student loan disbursement. There is no lack of worthy causes. The point is to choose one near and dear to your heart and commit to it.

BELOVED COMMUNITY AGREEMENTS

Over the years working in higher education and social justice, I have found that people of good will who come together still need guardrails for doing this work. Often, misunderstandings and ruptures arise among people who have different life experiences and worldviews. It's important to have a way to enable everyone present to stay at the table and work through our differences without hostility. I had a colleague who used to say, "With friends like these, who needs enemies?" As a group facilitator, I was often disappointed by our inability as a working group to get on the same page and focus on the issues at hand, though I, too, was guilty of getting sidetracked or distracted. These agreements are designed to help us, particularly when we're struggling to deepen our mutual understandings in difficult discussions or decisions. It's important to have agreements like these in place before we begin. It's hard to insert them in the middle of a heated argument. Even garnering the motivation to establish guidelines is a challenge. In my work, I found that people would seldom take copies of the agreements and use them beforehand, but after a difficult encounter, they often came back and asked for them. That reluctance exemplifies how difficult it is to acknowledge the vigilance required to do this work, even among people of good will. For example, in a group I worked with, we assumed everyone was on the same page politically, but a rupture occurred when one person, it turned out, had a very different political position. That rupture was never healed over the course of our ensuing time together. That person ended up leaving the group. Too often, these days, differences are so extreme, it's hard to work together even on things we do agree on. When we can agree to disagree about the stumbling blocks, it's easier for us to work together on other things. When extreme othering or demonizing happens, it's hard to restore good will. One way to avoid this dilemma is to pay particular attention to the nine principles listed below. One I find particularly useful is "call people *in* rather than *out*." Loretta Ross, a civil and reproductive rights activist, is known for this phrase.[5] It is extremely helpful in reducing ruptures and keeping things on track.

Groups don't have to use these specific agreements; they can create their own. But sometimes, it's easier to have them in advance and not spend the time reinventing them.

BELOVED COMMUNITY AGREEMENTS

How to engage in courageous dialogue across differences.

1. I step out of my comfort zone.
2. I use "I" statements.
3. I refrain from blaming, shaming, attacking, or discounting self or others.
4. I recognize that even good intentions may cause harm.
5. I call people *in* rather than *out*.
6. I go *in* instead of *on*.
7. I use my privilege in the service of others.
8. I make spaces safe for people to take risks.
9. I create opportunities for repair if things go awry.

CENTERING QUESTIONS

Centering questions help members of a group reflect on their own unconscious biases and behaviors that might get in the way of the work. Often, people want to jump right into problem solving. If we paid more attention at the outset to interpersonal and group dynamics, we might be more effective and save time in the long run. I've been told by committed activists that the issues we're tackling

5. Ross, *Calling In*, 9.

are so critical to the well-being of our communities, we can't afford to take time away from the work of helping people. But without focusing on *how* we get things done as well as *what* we do, the work can become more difficult and take longer.

I often ask people to identify something they do well and something they find challenging as they examine their own tendencies. I always start with myself—what I find I do well and what I find challenging. I'm good at giving the gift of my story and unpacking my own culture and identities. That's a strength. What I don't do well is harder to talk about, and I imagine this is true for most of us. I know I want to be better at listening and pausing before I react. I've had a lot of training in listening well. However, I often find myself thinking about how I want to respond while someone else is talking rather than listening deeply. I am often surprised at the vulnerability people exhibit as they consider these questions, which are designed to help foster trust and humility.

CENTERING QUESTIONS (AUTHOR UNKNOWN)[6]

What space do I take up? Am I putting myself at the center?

Do I apologize too much? When I do, am I making it about me?

Do I give the gift of my story? Do I unpack the cultures, identities, and experiences that made me who I am? Do I receive the gift of others' stories?

Am I denying my own reality? Am I denying the reality of others?

Am I honest with myself about what I don't know? Do I make assumptions when I should be asking questions?

Do I actually listen? Do I pause before I react?

Am I defensive? All-knowing? Performative?

Have I committed to reading, learning, and growing?

6. These were given to me some time ago on a handout on which it said, "Author Unknown."

Am I willing to do the humble, painful work of learning, unlearning, relearning over and over?

COVENANT OF NONVIOLENCE

A commitment to nonviolence is at least as important today as it was during the civil rights era. It's important for moral reasons, but it's also the case that perceptions matter. Violence at demonstrations, seen on national media, erodes public support. Burning cars and throwing rocks and bottles diverts attention from the issues at hand. The goal is to win people's hearts and minds and get them to understand what's at stake. Public demonstrations are generally peaceful. It's those who come with a deliberate intention of disruption, often later in the day, who give demonstrators a bad name. The challenge is how to prevent outside provocateurs from turning them violent or destructive. In a few instances with Black Lives Matter, demonstrators have turned those disrupters over to the police as a way of saying, "They're not with us. We don't condone this."[7]

I don't think we have satisfactory solutions regarding how we handle this, but we need to make every effort to keep the focus on the issue, not the destruction that follows in the wake of some demonstrations. This covenant is an excellent way to hold ourselves accountable. The Poor People's Campaign has created a covenant as a way to maintain the focus and integrity of a protest. So many more people would demonstrate and be in the streets if they felt they could count on an orderly process. It's important to have an intergenerational movement. The Poor People's Campaign talks about fusion politics, which includes a wide array of people from all races, economic backgrounds, and ages.[8] In order to bring about the change we want, it helps to have a broad cross-section of people involved. I participated in a Moral Monday demonstration led by the Poor People's Campaign and was inspired to do much more and to stay engaged. It was very well organized and there

7. WFLA 8, "'Agitator' Apprehended by Protesters."

8. https://www.poorpeoplescampaign.org.

was training regarding what to do in confrontational situations with the police. Demonstrators were instructed to step back when the police told them to if they didn't want to get arrested, and, if they were willing to be arrested, to go peacefully. Volunteers have been trained how to support people who are arrested by calling family members, maintaining a log of arrests, arranging bail, and identifying other needs. Those who have outstanding warrants are discouraged from risking arrest. For most who have clear records, charges are likely to be quietly dropped.

The New Poor People's Campaign has restored a spiritual and moral dimension that is sometimes missing in social and political movements. The spiritual component of the civil rights movement kept us on track. Events like Moral Mondays not only encourage participants and build community; they can be spiritually healing and inspiring. The demonstration I attended helped me decide to pursue a seminary education late in life because I wanted to have a strong moral fabric and to use the scriptures for good where others were using them for contentious purposes.

POOR PEOPLE'S CAMPAIGN COVENANT OF NONVIOLENCE

(Used by permission of The Poor People's Campaign.)

This Covenant of Nonviolence draws on lessons from historic nonviolent social movements and our experiences in building this Campaign. At all our activities, events and actions, we seek to uphold the following principles:

1. **I will act with respect towards all.** Nonviolence is a way of life for courageous people. It is active resistance to the interlocking injustices we face every day. It requires presence of mind and a profound moral and spiritual commitment to ending injustice. I will maintain my presence of mind and walk with dignity in my actions.

2. **I will speak truth to power.** Nonviolence seeks to win friendship and understanding. I will confront those who disagree with our position using grace, intelligence, truth and compassion and never compromise my principles.
3. **I will seek to defeat injustice, not people.** Nonviolence recognizes that we are all impacted by the systemic root causes of injustice. I will not humiliate my opponent but call forth the good in them and challenge them and our society to live up to our true potential.
4. **I will accept the consequences of my actions for justice.** Nonviolence prepares us to accept the consequences of our actions without retaliation and to not respond violently even to acts of violence.
5. **I will not resist arrest, use hostile language or insults, carry or use weapons or make any threats of violence.**
6. **I will walk in love.** Nonviolence resists violence of both the body and the spirit and demands that we love our neighbor. Nonviolent love is active, spontaneous, unselfish and generous, giving willingly even when it may be returned with hostility.
7. **I may wear a face mask for the health and safety of myself and others.** However, I will not otherwise obstruct my ability to tell my story about why the PPC is important to me in a public and accessible manner.
8. **I believe the universe is on the side of justice.** Nonviolence is rooted in the belief that justice will ultimately win against injustice. All of history is moving us in this direction.
9. **I am committed to a movement, not a moment.** The changes we seek require long hours of work, strength, courage, creativity and commitment to an effort that is beyond any individual. Nonviolence compels us to act in community, to learn with and from others, to build fusion unity across lines of division, including race, ethnicity, class, sexual orientation, immigration and documentation status, gender and gender

identity, and to prioritize the leadership and demands of those most impacted by the injustices we face.

10. **In committing to these principles, I will tap into a power and soul force that exists within each of us.** I will be firmly grounded in nonviolence as a philosophy, practice, and moral and spiritual discipline. I will strive to embody the values of courage, inclusion, justice, truth and love for all that connect me to every human being.

WHAT CAN WE DO BETTER?

We are living in a moment of both hope and despair. We are called on to decide which we will focus on. A Native American folk story about two wolves describes that the wolf who wins depends on which you feed[9]. These practices can help us focus on the good in each other and lift us out of the despair so many are feeling. They can remind us that there is more to life than what we may be reacting to. Even though we live in the here and now, our lives go on forever.

1. Listen to understand, not just with our heads but with our hearts.
2. Ask nonjudgmental questions.
3. Ask ourselves how things would be different if we were able to embrace the changes we find uncomfortable.
4. Tell our stories, including mistakes and failures.
5. Create communal spaces and intergenerational families (not necessarily blood relatives) of like-minded people who can live and work together for each other's highest good.
6. Challenge and change the structures that perpetuate war, poverty, and racism.
7. Embrace religion and spirituality in new ways.

9. Ilagan, "Story of the Two Wolves."

Former President Barack Obama borrowed the words "*Yes, we can—Si, se puede*" from the Farm Workers' Movement for labor rights led by César Chavez and Dolores Huerta.[10] This was the saying that fueled his campaign and gave America hope that we could rise above what some people call America's greatest sin and elect a Black man as president of the United States. Although we accomplished that, we still have unfinished business in the work of creating a more perfect union.

10. Obama, "Yes We Can."

Bibliography

Allen, James. *Without Sanctuary: Lynching Photography in America.* Sante Fe, NM: Twin Palms, 1999.

Anderson, Lydia, et al. "Share of One-Person Households More Than Tripled from 1940 to 2020." United States Census Bureau, June 8, 2023. https://www.census.gov/library/stories/2023/06/more-than-a-quarter-all-households-have-one-person.html

Beloved Community Center. "Greensboro Truth and Reconciliation Commission Project." https://belovedcommunitycenter.org/greensboro-truth-reconciliation-commission-project/.

Boggs, Grace Lee. "A Conspiracy of Hope: The Beloved Community of Martin Luther King." *Yes!*, May 21, 2004. https://www.yesmagazine.org/issue/hope-conspiracy/2004/05/21/the-beloved-community-of-martin-luther-king.

Burrow, Rufus. *God and Human Dignity: The Personalism, Theology, and Ethics of Martin Luther King, Jr.* University of Notre Dame Press, 2006.

Center for the Preservation of Civil Rights Sites. "Highlander Research and Education Center." https://cpcrs.upenn.edu/resource/highlander-research-and-education-center.

The Choir Room. "Hi, We're the Choir Room." https://www.choirisback.com/about.

Clayborn Historic Temple. "Our Story." https://clayborn.org/about-us/.

Crossroads Antiracism Organizing and Training. "Continuum on Becoming an Anti-Racist Multicultural Organization." https://www.cacgrants.org/assets/ce/Documents/Continuum.pdf.

Elliot, Debbie. "Wallace in the Schoolhouse Door." NPR Morning Edition, June 11, 2003. https://www.npr.org/2003/06/11/1294680/wallace-in-the-schoolhouse-door.

Frost, Robert. *The Poetry of Robert Frost.* Holt, Rinehart & Winston, 1969.

Gandhi, M. K. *Non-Violent Resistance (Satyagraha).* New York: Schocken, 1961.

Gospel Music Association. "Old Church Basement from Elevation Worship and Maverick City Music Makes History Its First Week of Release." May 11, 2021. https://gospelmusic.org/news/old-church-basement-from-elevation-worship-and-maverick-city-music-makes-history-its-first-week-of-release.

Greene, David, and John Erman, dirs. *Roots*. "Part 2," written by William Blinn and Ernest Kinoy. Aired Jan. 24, 1977 on ABC.

Haley, Alex. *Roots: The Saga of an American Family*. Doubleday, 1976.

Harding, Vincent. *Martin Luther King: The Inconvenient Hero*. Orbis, 2013.

Girma, Haben. *Haben: The Deafblind Woman Who Conquered Harvard Law*. Twelve, 2019.

Hamer, Fanny Lou. "Testimony at the Democratic National Convention 1964," Atlantic City, NJ. Aug. 22, 1964.

Hankey, Kate. "I Love to Tell the Story." In *Methodist Hymnal*, 156. Nashville: United Methodist, 1989.

Hoffman, Deborah, and Frances Reid, dirs. *Long Night's Journey Into Day*. Los Angeles: Seventh Art Releasing, 2000.

Holben, Lawrence. *What Christians Think About Homosexuality: Six Representative Viewpoints*. D&F Scott, 1999.

Ilagan, Gabrielle. "The Story of the Two Wolves." Manhattan Center for CBT, November 3, 2025. https://manhattancbt.com/story-of-the-two-wolves/.

Isserman, Maurice. "Saving the Soul of America." Religious Socialism, April 3, 2017. https://www.religioussocialism.org/saving_the_soul_of_america_1967.

Jackson, Bailey W. "Theory and Practice of Multicultural Organization Development." In *The NTL Handbook of Organization Development and Change*, edited by Brenda B. Jones and Michael Brazzel, 139–54. Pfeiffer, 2006.

Jaynes, Gerald D., ed. "Literacy." In *Encyclopedia of African American Society*, 505. Thousand Oaks, CA: SAGE, 2005. https://doi.org/10.4135/9781412952507.n384.

Jones, Jeffrey. "Church Attendance Has Declined in Most U.S. Religious Groups." Gallup, Mar. 25, 2024. https://news.gallup.com/poll/642548/church-attendance-declined-religious-groups.aspx.

King, Martin Luther, Jr. "Address at the Thirty-Sixth Annual Dinner of the War Resisters League." New York, NY. Feb. 2, 1959.

———. "Beyond Vietnam: Breaking the Silence." Riverside Church, New York. April 4, 1967.

———. "The Drum-Major Instinct." Ebenezer Baptist Church, Atlanta, GA. Feb. 4, 1968.

———. "I Have a Dream." March on Washington for Jobs and Freedom, Washington, DC. Aug. 28, 1963.

———. "I've Been to the Mountaintop." Mason Temple, Memphis, TN. April 3, 1968.

———. "Letter from Birmingham Jail." Apr. 16, 1963. https://www.learningforjustice.org/sites/default/files/general/Letter%20from%20Birmingham%20Jail%20MLK.pdf.

———. "Suffering and Faith." *Christian Century*, Apr. 27, 1960. https://kinginstitute.stanford.edu/king-papers/documents/suffering-and-faith.

———. "Where Do We Go from Here?" Southern Christian Leadership Conference, Atlanta, GA. August 16, 1967.

Lee, Danny. "Haben Girma: My Disability Has Been an Opportunity for Innovation." *Guardian*, Dec. 19, 2019. https://www.theguardian.com/society/2019/dec/17/haben-girma-deafblind-disability-opportunity-innovation.

Lee, Hak Joon. "To Save the Soul of America: Martin Luther King, Jr. and the Renewal of America Today." Reformed Journal, Mar. 1, 2008. https://reformedjournal.com/2008/03/01/to-save-the-soul-of-america-martin-luther-king-jr-and-the-renewal-of-america-today/.

Lewis, John. *Across That Bridge: Life Lessons and a Vision for Change.* Legacy, 2012.

———. "Edmund Pettus Bridge Address." American Rhetoric, Mar. 7, 2015. https://www.americanrhetoric.com/speeches/johnlewisedmundpettusbridgespeech.htm.

Mayer, Deanna Wiley. "From Fear to Truth." *Sojourners*, Feb. 2006. https://sojo.net/magazine/february-2006/fear-truth.

McCoy, Byron F., ed. *Zion Still Sings*. Pew ed. Abingdon, 1981.

McWhorter, Diane. *Carry Me Home*. Simon & Schuster, 2001.

Myers, Verna. *Moving Diversity Forward: How to Go from Well-Meaning to Well-Doing*. American Bar Association, 2011.

Obama, Barack. "Barack Obama: Yes We Can." Nashua, NH, Jan. 8, 2009. YouTube video, 13:09. https://www.youtube.com/watch?v=Fe751kMBwms.

Parachin, Janet. *Engaged Spirituality: Lives of Contemplation and Action.* Chalice, 1999.

Romero, Roselyn. "West Oakland's 7th Street Was Once a Black Cultural Hub. A New Plan Aims to Restore It." Oaklandside, Oct. 16, 2023. https://oaklandside.org/2023/10/16/7th-street-development-west-oakland-thrives-revitalization-report/.

Ross, Loretta. *Calling In: How to Start Making Change with Those You'd Rather Cancel*. Simon & Schuster, 2025.

Royce, Josiah. *The Problem of Christianity*. Vol. 1. New York: MacMillan, 1913.

Summers, Juana. "Survivors of 1921 Tulsa Race Massacre Share Eyewitness Accounts." NPR, Mar. 19, 2021. https://www.npr.org/2021/05/19/998225207/survivors-of-1921-tulsa-race-massacre-share-eyewitness-accounts.

Susaneck, Adam Paul. "Segregation by Design." TU Delft Centre for the Just City, 2024. https://www.segregationbydesign.com/

Thomas, Frank. "Can We Be Friends?" Christian Theological Seminary, Indianapolis, IN. Sept. 10, 2014.

Thurman, Howard. *The Growing Edge*. Richmond, IN: Friends United, 1956.

Wallace, George C. "Inaugural Address of Governor George C. Wallace." State Capitol, Montgomery, AL. Jan. 14, 1963.

West, Cornell. "Ware Lecture." Unitarian Universalist Association, General Assembly 215, Portland, OR. June 27, 2015.

WFLA 8. "Watch: 'Agitator' Apprehended by Protesters, Handed Over to Police." June 1, 2020. https://www.wjbf.com/newsfeed-now/watch-agitator-apprehended-by-protesters-handed-over-to-police/#.

Zimmerman, Kristin Lynn. *Ten Thousand Beloved Communities*. Oakland, CA: Beloved Communities Network, 2023.